DATE DUE			
JE 10 '9			

PRAIRIE DOGS

UNUSUAL ANIMALS

Lynn M. Stone

The Rourke Corporation, Inc.
Vero Beach, Florida 32964

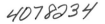

Edited by Sandra A. Robinson

PHOTO CREDITS
All photos © Lynn M. Stone except page 12 © Breck Kent

Library of Congress Cataloging-in-Publication Data

Stone, Lynn M.
 Prairie dogs / by Lynn M. Stone.
  p. cm. — (Unusual animals)
 Includes index.
 Summary: Examines the physical characteristics, habits, and
distinctive towns of the prairie dog.
 ISBN 0-86593-282-4
 1. Prairie dogs—Juvenile literature. [1. Prairie dogs.]
I. Title. II. Series: Stone, Lynn M. Unusual animals.
QL737.R68S75   1993
599.32'32—dc20   93-19463
                                                            CIP
                                                            AC

TABLE OF CONTENTS

The Unusual Prairie Dogs   5
Prairie Dog Cousins   6
Where Prairie Dogs Live   9
Prairie Dog Towns   11
What Prairie Dogs Eat   14
The Prairie Dog's Enemies   16
Baby Prairie Dogs   19
Prairie Dog Habits   20
Prairie Dogs and People   22
Glossary   23
Index   24

THE UNUSUAL PRAIRIE DOGS

Prairie dogs "bark," but they are not dogs at all. They are plump ground squirrels with short legs and short, twitchy tails.

It's not just a curious name that makes the prairie dog unusual. Unlike other squirrels, prairie dogs live in huge "dog towns." Sometimes thousands of prairie dogs dig their burrows in a single town. Prairie dogs not only live close together, they protect and take care of each other. They are unusually **social** animals.

A black-tailed prairie dog yips
   from the door of its burrow

PRAIRIE DOG COUSINS

Prairie dogs and their closest cousins, the squirrels, are **rodents.** Rodents are **gnawing,** or chewing, animals. Many rodents are already familiar to you—mice, rats, beavers and woodchucks, for example.

Rodents such as porcupines and beavers chew wood. Prairie dogs do most of their chewing on the plants they eat.

Several **species,** or kinds, of squirrels live on and under the ground, as prairie dogs do. The smallest ground squirrels are chipmunks. The largest are woodchucks and marmots.

Marmots of the Western mountains are the largest of the ground squirrels

WHERE PRAIRIE DOGS LIVE

Four species of prairie dogs live on the open, grassy lands, or prairies, of several Western states and two Canadian provinces.

The black-tailed prairie dog, the most common species, lives from southern Alberta and Saskatchewan south to Texas.

Three types of prairie dogs with white tails—the Utah, Gunnison's and white-tailed—live in scattered dog towns from Montana south to New Mexico and Arizona.

A fifth species, the Mexican prairie dog, lives in northeastern Mexico.

Dawn spreads over a buffalo herd in South Dakota's prairie dog country

PRAIRIE DOG TOWNS

Prairie dog towns and the tunnels within them are amazing places. A tunnel may be more than 100 feet long. The main tunnel has branch tunnels that lead to the prairie dog's toilet and nest.

In the past, one black-tailed prairie dog town might have covered more land than the state of Rhode Island. Towns of that size may have had as many as 400 million "dogs"! Prairie dog towns today are much smaller.

A buffalo cow stops to nurse her calf while visiting a prairie dog town

Utah white-tailed prairie dogs have become endangered

A black-tailed prairie dog barks an alarm before scurrying into its burrow

WHAT PRAIRIE DOGS EAT

Prairie dogs are little lawn mowers as well as digging machines. They dine mostly on flowers and grasses as they graze around their burrows. Sometimes prairie dogs mix grasshoppers and other insects into their diets.

Prairie dogs trim their little pastures close to the ground. That helps them keep a better lookout for **predators,** the animals that hunt them.

Using its front paws like hands, a prairie dog snacks on prairie greens

THE PRAIRIE DOG'S ENEMIES

Prairie dogs are **prey,** or food, for several predators—coyotes, foxes, badgers, hawks, eagles and snakes. The black-footed ferret, a relative of otters and weasels, once lived entirely on prairie dogs. However, black-footed ferrets have nearly disappeared, or become **extinct.**

Prairie dogs have excellent hearing and eyesight to help them escape from predators. Prairie dogs help each other by barking warnings from the dirt mounds by their burrows.

A hungry bull snake makes a "house call" at a prairie dog burrow

BABY PRAIRIE DOGS

A mother prairie dog has a litter of three to five babies each spring. Black-tailed prairie dogs are raised as part of a small group within the town. The group is made up of several young, three or four adult females, and an adult male.

A young prairie dog stays with the family until it is two years old. By then it is old enough to begin its own family.

Young prairie dogs explore the green world at the edge of their burrow

PRAIRIE DOG HABITS

Prairie dogs nap deep in their burrows during cold weather. White-tailed prairie dogs slip into a deep sleep called **hibernation.** Black-tailed prairie dogs sleep much of winter away, but they sometimes pop out of their burrows.

Black-tailed prairie dogs are especially friendly to each other. They nuzzle, **groom**—clean—each other and play together.

Prairie dogs spend hours mending tunnels and the dirt mounds at burrow entrances.

A prairie dog mother grooms her youngster

PRAIRIE DOGS AND PEOPLE

Prairie dogs eat some of the same grasses that cattle do, so prairie dogs have never been popular with ranchers. With government help, ranchers have poisoned millions of prairie dogs to save grasses for cattle. Since 1900, the number of prairie dogs in Texas has dropped from 800 million to less than 3 million.

Prairie dogs have disappeared in large numbers from other areas, too. The Utah and Mexican prairie dogs are **endangered**—in danger of disappearing forever.

Glossary

endangered (en DANE jerd) — in danger of no longer existing; very rare

extinct (ex TINKT) — no longer existing

gnawing (NAW ing) — having the ability to nibble something away by steady chewing

groom (GROOM) — to clean and straighten fur or feathers

hibernation (hi bur NAY shun) — the sleeplike state in which certain animals survive winter

predator (PRED uh tor) — an animal that kills other animals for food

prey (PRAY) — an animal that is hunted for food by another animal

rodent (RO dent) — a large group of gnawing mammals

social (SO shul) — spending considerable time in the company of others of the same kind

species (SPEE sheez) — within a group of closely-related living things, such as prairie dogs, one certain kind or type (*black-tailed* prairie dog)

INDEX

babies   19
beavers   6
burrows   5, 16, 20
cattle   22
chipmunks   6
dog towns   5, 9, 11
eyesight   16
ferret, black-footed   16
flowers   14
grasses   14, 22
ground squirrels   5, 6
hearing   16
hibernation   20
insects   14
legs   5
litter   19
marmots   6
mice   6
nest   11

plants   6
porcupines   6
prairie dog
   black-tailed   9, 11, 19, 20
   Gunnison's   9
   Mexican   9, 22
   Utah   9, 22
   white-tailed   9, 20
predators   14, 16
prey   16
ranchers   22
rats   6
rodents   6
species   6
squirrels   5, 6
tails   5
Texas   9, 22
tunnels   11, 20
woodchucks   6